# The Things We Throw Away

Focus: Recycling

Meredith Costain

Every week we throw
out the trash. Most of the
trash comes from things
we buy.

Not all things we buy are made to last. Some things we only use once. Then we throw them away.

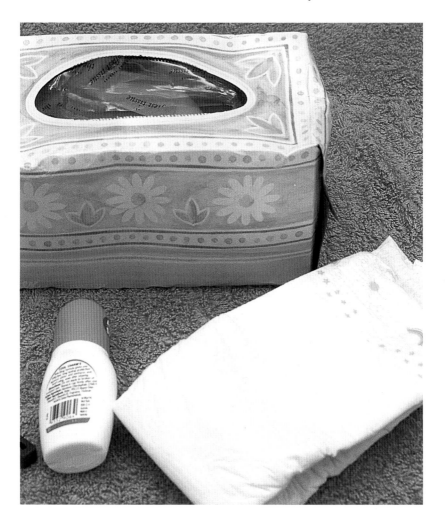

Things we buy are wrapped in packaging. We take off the packaging and throw it away.

People have studied trash. They wanted to know what kind of things we throw away.

Most trash is packaging. We throw away lots of paper wrappers. We throw away paper bags and cardboard boxes.

Some of our trash is plastic.
We throw away plastic
bags and plastic bottles.
Sometimes we throw away
broken plastic toys.

Some of our trash is metal. We throw away metal cans. We throw away metal foil. Sometimes we throw away broken metal forks.

Some of our trash is glass.
We throw away glass bottles.
We throw away glass jars.
Sometimes we throw away
broken light bulbs.

Some of our trash is food scraps. We throw away banana skins and potato peels. We throw away old lettuce. Sometimes we throw away food we don't like.

We used to send all of our trash to the dump. Dumps are dirty and smelly. Our dumps are also getting full. Soon there will be no place to dump our trash.

We can help. We can make less trash. We can put used paper, glass, and plastic in a recycling bin. Recycled trash can be made into new things.

We can put food scraps on a compost heap. The food scraps will become compost. We can use the compost to help us grow new food.

We can buy things that don't have much packaging. Fruit has its own packaging!

We can use things again.
An old milk carton can
become a plant's new home.

# What could we do with this trash?

# THE DAY WE MET